Nelson Mandela

Jennifer Strand

abdopublishing.com

Published by Abdo Zoom™, PO Box 398166, Minneapolis, Minnesota 55439. Copyright © 2017 by Abdo Consulting Group, Inc. International copyrights reserved in all countries. No part of this book may be reproduced in any form without written permission from the publisher. Abdo Zoom™ is a trademark and logo of Abdo Consulting Group, Inc.

Printed in the United States of America, North Mankato, Minnesota
072016
092016

THIS BOOK CONTAINS
RECYCLED MATERIALS

Cover Photo: Theana Calitz-Bilt/AP Images
Interior Photos: Theana Calitz-Bilt/AP Images, 1; Ron Frehm/AP Images, 5; Chris Van Lennep Photo/iStockphoto, 6–7; Apic/Getty Images, 7; API/Gamma-Rapho/Getty Images, 8; Schalk van Zuydam/AP Images, 10–11; Greg English/AP Images, 12; Amy Sancetta/AP Images, 13; John Eeg, File/AP Images, 14; John Parkin/AP Images, 15; Ed Bailey/AP Images, 16; Gallo Images/Rex Features/AP Images, 17; Walter Dhladhla/AFP/Getty Images, 18; George Clerk/iStockphoto, 19

Editor: Brienna Rossiter
Series Designer: Madeline Berger
Art Direction: Dorothy Toth

Publisher's Cataloging-in-Publication Data
Names: Strand, Jennifer, author.
Title: Nelson Mandela / by Jennifer Strand.
Description: Minneapolis, MN : Abdo Zoom, [2017] | Series: Legendary leaders
  | Includes bibliographical references and index.
Identifiers: LCCN 2016941379 | ISBN 9781680792393 (lib. bdg.) |
  ISBN 9781680794076 (ebook) | 9781680794960 (Read-to-me ebook)
Subjects: LCSH: Mandela, Nelson, 1918-2013--Juvenile literature. | Presidents--
  South Africa--Biography--Juvenile literature. | Political prisoners--South
  Africa--Biography--Juvenile literature. | Anti-apartheid activists--South
  Africa--Biography--Juvenile literature.
Classification: DDC 968.06/5092 [B]--dc23
LC record available at http://lccn.loc.gov/2016941379

Table of Contents

Introduction

Nelson Mandela was an activist. He helped end apartheid in South Africa.

He was also South Africa's first black president.

Early Life

Nelson was born on July 18, 1918. He lived in a small village. Later he went to live with the leader of his tribe.

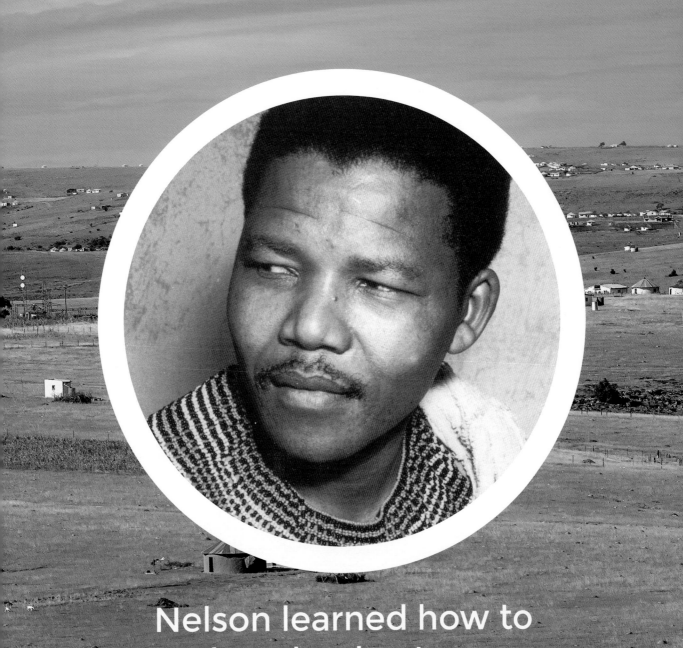

Nelson learned how to
be a leader, too.

Leader

8

Mandela wanted to help people be treated fairly. He worked to end apartheid. He led **protests**.

The government did not want to change. It sent Mandela to jail. He was in jail for 27 years.

But he kept working.

Mandela was set free in 1990.

He worked with South Africa's president. They helped make the government fairer.

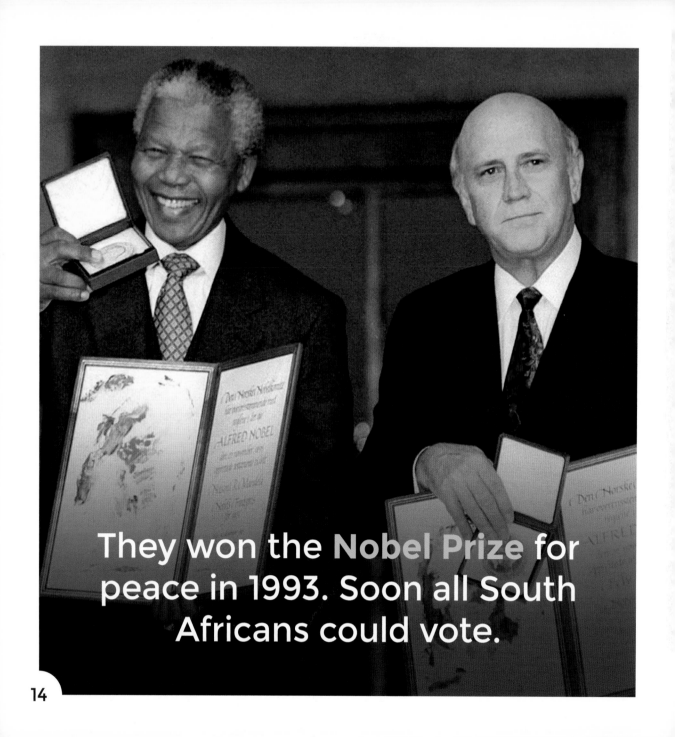

They won the **Nobel Prize** for peace in 1993. Soon all South Africans could vote.

They picked Mandela
to be president.

Legacy

Mandela was president until 1999.

He helped bring his country together. He also tried to help poor people.

Mandela died on
December 5, 2013.

People around the
world admired him.

Nelson Mandela

Born: July 18, 1918

Birthplace: Mvezo, Transkei, South Africa

Known For: Mandela was an activist. He helped end apartheid. He was the first black president of South Africa.

Died: December 5, 2013

Key Dates

1918: Rolihlahla Mandela is born on July 18.

1925: Mandela's teacher gives him the name "Nelson."

1964–1990: Mandela is in jail.

1993: Mandela and F. W. de Klerk win the Nobel Peace Prize.

1994–1999: Mandela is president of South Africa.

2013: Mandela dies on December 5.

Glossary

activist - a person who works for change.

apartheid - a system in South Africa that did not give black people the same rights as white people.

Nobel Prize - an important award given out each year.

protest - an event where people show they oppose something.

tribe - a group of people who share the same culture and beliefs.

Booklinks

For more information
on **Nelson Mandela**, please visit
booklinks.abdopublishing.com

Zoom In on Biographies!

Learn even more with the Abdo Zoom
Biographies database. Check out
abdozoom.com for more information.

Index